REALITY
TV
TITANS

FUN AND FOOD WITH
Guy Fieri

Jill C. Wheeler

**Checkerboard
Library**

An Imprint of Abdo Publishing
abdopublishing.com

abdopublishing.com

Published by Abdo Publishing, a division of ABDO, PO Box 398166, Minneapolis, Minnesota 55439.
Copyright © 2016 by Abdo Consulting Group, Inc. International copyrights reserved in all countries.
No part of this book may be reproduced in any form without written permission from the publisher.
Checkerboard Library™ is a trademark and logo of Abdo Publishing.

Printed in the United States of America, North Mankato, Minnesota

062015
092015

THIS BOOK CONTAINS
RECYCLED MATERIALS

Design: Jen Schoeller, Mighty Media, Inc.
Production: Christa Schneider, Mighty Media, Inc.
Series Editor: Liz Salzmann
Cover Photos: AP Images, cover; Shutterstock, back cover
Interior Photos: AP Images, pp. 5, 17, 23; Corbis, pp. 13, 21; Corbis/AP Images, p. 15; Photo courtesy
Ferndale (CA) Museum collection. Used with permission, pp. 6, 8; Mighty Media, Inc., p. 25;
Shutterstock, pp. 3, 7, 9 11, 12, 19, 27, 29

Library of Congress Cataloging-in-Publication Data

Wheeler, Jill C., 1964-
  Fun and food with Guy Fieri / Jill C. Wheeler.
      pages cm. -- (Reality TV titans)
  Includes index.
  ISBN 978-1-62403-817-4
1. Fieri, Guy--Juvenile literature. 2. Cooks--California--Biography--Juvenile literature I. Title.
  TX649.F485W44 2016
  641.5092--dc23
  [B]
                          2015005953

CONTENTS

Guy Fieri	4
California Kid	6
Pretzel Pusher	8
Guy in France	10
New Adventures	12
Restaurateur	14
TV Debut	16
Triple D	18
Touring Fun	20
More on the Menu	22
Home & Family	24
Giving Back	26
Timeline	28
Guy Fieri Says	28
Glossary	30
Websites	31
Index	32

Guy Fieri

Guy Fieri is part chef, part rock star. He wears skateboarding shorts, bowling shirts, and flip-flops instead of a chef's jacket and hat. His spiked blond hair and wraparound sunglasses are often seen on the Food Network. Fieri's *Diners, Drive-ins and Dives* is one of the network's most popular shows.

Fieri never attended **culinary** school, but he has written several popular cookbooks of original recipes. He has also written books about his experiences on *Diners, Drive-ins and Dives*. Several of his books have been on *The New York Times* Best Sellers list.

Fieri believes food is a natural connection among people everywhere. His fans love the way he blends different **cuisines** from around the world. He enjoys featuring everyday food that satisfies the soul as well as the taste buds.

DID YOU KNOW?
Fieri has at least 20 tattoos.

Fieri believes cooking can be fun and exciting.

California Kid

Guy Fieri was born on January 22, 1968, in Columbus, Ohio. His name was Guy Ramsey Ferry. He was Jim and Penny Ferry's first child. Guy's younger sister, Morgan, was born four years later.

Guy's second-grade school photo

Guy's grandfather was Giuseppe Fieri. He moved to the United States from Italy. Like many **immigrants**, he changed the spelling of the family name. Guy later changed his name to the original spelling in honor of his Italian ancestry.

The Ferry family moved to California when Guy was a baby. They eventually settled in the small northern California

Main Street in Ferndale, California, where Guy grew up

town of Ferndale. Young Guy was full of energy. His mother compares his childhood to a three-ring circus! Like many boys, Guy dreamed of becoming a race car driver or a rock star. He enjoyed skateboarding and camping.

But Guy would discover another activity that he loved. Guy's parents cooked **vegetarian**, non-dairy, whole grain foods. But Guy wanted something different to eat. So when he was 10 years old, he started learning to cook.

Pretzel Pusher

Guy's first job in the food business was running a lemonade stand. But he got a better idea while on a family ski trip. He loved the soft pretzels at California's Squaw Valley Ski Resort. He remembers eating up to ten at a time! His father asked Guy if he would like his own pretzel cart. Guy said yes.

Guy Fieri sells Awesome Pretzels at the Foggy Bottom Milk Run in Ferndale.

The two created a plan for the business. To get started, Guy needed to learn which company made his favorite pretzels. But the man selling them wouldn't tell him. So Guy looked in the ski resort's trash. He found the company's name on an empty pretzel box!

After returning home, Guy and his father built a

three-wheeled bicycle pushcart. Guy named his business The Awesome Pretzel. He sold pretzels to neighbors and at local events for six years. The business earned enough money for Guy to pursue another dream.

Guy in France

During Guy's youth, his family hosted several exchange students and foreign guests. Guy wanted to be an exchange student too. Guy got his chance when he was in high school. One evening, his parents had a man from France over for dinner. He offered to find Guy a place to live in France. Guy's mother said he could go.

His mother's consent had one condition. Guy had to take a French class first. He needed to earn at least a B. Guy took a French class at a nearby college. He met his mother's expectations and finished the class with a B. When he was 16 years old, he flew to Chantilly, France.

In Chantilly, Guy lived in a third-floor room. It just had a bed and a sink. There were times when France was not what Guy expected. But he knew he had to make the best of things.

Guy soon learned to better speak French. He also learned about international food. As a chef, Guy is not known for French food. Yet French **cuisine** was his first love. His experiences in France led to his career in the **culinary** arts.

The French town Guy lived in is famous for its Chantilly cream, a sweet dessert topping.

New Adventures

After 11 months in France, Fieri returned to the United States. After high school, he went to the University of Nevada, Las Vegas. There, studied the hotel and restaurant business. Fieri did not study cooking in particular. However, he worked at several restaurants while taking classes. He graduated in 1990 with a degree in **hospitality** management.

Fieri's first job after college was managing a Stouffer's restaurant in Long Beach, California. He worked there three years. Then he became the district manager of a restaurant chain called Louise's Trattoria.

Around this time, Fieri met Lori Brisson. They got married in 1995. Guy and Lori Fieri would go on to have two sons, Hunter in 1996, and Ryder in 2005.

The University of Nevada, Las Vegas, where Fieri earned his college degree

Hunter, Lori, Guy, and Ryder Fieri

Restaurateur

Fieri wanted to open his own restaurant. He met Steven Gruber at Louise's Trattoria. They worked together there. They became friends and decided to be business partners.

In 1996, they opened a restaurant in Santa Rosa, California. It was called Johnny Garlic's California Pasta Grill. It was very successful. Soon there were additional locations. But Fieri and Gruber didn't stop there.

In 1999, they opened a different kind of restaurant. It was a Southern barbeque and California-style sushi restaurant. They called it Tex Wasabi's Rock n' Roll Sushi BBQ. It was also in Santa Rosa. They opened a second Tex Wasabi's in Sacramento, California, in 2007.

The Sacramento Tex Wasabi's closed in 2013, but the one in Santa Rosa is still open. And as of 2015, there were seven Johnny Garlic's restaurants.

DID YOU KNOW?
The only food Fieri won't eat is beef liver.

Guy's American Kitchen & Bar in New York City is Fieri's eleventh restaurant.

In 2012, Fieri expanded to the East Coast. He opened Guy's American Kitchen & Bar in New York, New York. He made plans to open restaurants in other cities as well.

TV Debut

The success of his restaurants showed Fieri's **culinary** ability was top-notch. In 2005, Fieri's friends urged him to enter *The Next Food Network Star*. It is a Food Network competition series. He agreed.

Fieri sent his videotaped entry to the Food Network. More than 1,000 others also entered. The judges were impressed with Fieri's energy and on-camera presence. He was chosen as a **finalist**. They invited Fieri to come to New York, New York, for the next step.

Fieri wasn't sure he should go. It was right before Christmas. He didn't want to be away from his family and his restaurants. Plus, he and his wife were expecting their second child. But Lori insisted that he go.

Fieri was one of eight finalists. It took three weeks to tape the show. They taped interviews, cooking, and other activities. The **episodes** aired over a three-month period. The final episode

DID YOU KNOW?
On a Food Network clip, Fieri says that if he were a food, he'd be lasagna.

Fieri at Food Network's twentieth birthday party in October 2013

was shown on April 23, 2006. Fieri won the contest! The prize was six **episodes** of his own cooking show. His show was called *Guy's Big Bite* and it first aired on June 25, 2006. It showcased flavors as big and bold as the host. *Guy's Big Bite* was a huge success.

17

Triple D

In November 2006, Fieri hosted a special called *Diners, Drive-ins and Dives*. Fieri calls it "Triple D." In the program, Fieri hit the road. He drove a red 1967 Chevy Camaro Super Sport convertible. He visited small restaurants around the country. He sampled each restaurant's specialties. *Diners, Drive-ins and Dives* was just going to be one **episode**. But in April 2007, it became a regular show.

Food Network crew members arrive at the restaurants before Fieri. For each episode of Triple D, the team films many more minutes than they need. This is edited down to about seven to eight minutes per restaurant. Most half-hour episodes feature three locations.

During the show, Fieri asks the restaurant owners to share their stories. His natural curiosity and love of food bring the different stories to life. Fieri is happy to peek inside cooking pots, ask questions, and chat with customers. He also takes pride in what the show can do for the restaurants. Many of them became much more popular after a visit from Triple D.

Fieri spray-paints a self-portrait on the wall of each diner he visits for Triple D.

Touring Fun

Fieri drives a red convertible on Triple D. He doesn't own the *Diners, Drive-ins and Dives* car. But he is a classic car collector. As of 2015, his collection included a 1968 Pontiac Firebird, a 1971 Chevy Chevelle, and a 1976 Jeep CJ-5.

In 2009, Fieri went on a national tour. "The Guy Fieri Road Show" toured 21 cities. It featured music and drinks as well as cooking **demonstrations**. It was half cooking demonstration, half rock **concert**.

For Fieri, food and music is a natural mix. He has always loved music. He even keeps a drum set in his kitchen! He is friends with many musicians including Kid Rock and Sammy Hagar. Fieri enjoys playing drums and keyboards. But he knows he's not good enough to quit his day job!

DID YOU KNOW?
Most of Fieri's classic cars are bright yellow.

Fieri at the House of Blues in Las Vegas in 2009. It was the last stop of "The Guy Fieri Road Show."

More on the Menu

Fieri has released products to support both his shows and his personal brand. He published his first book in 2008. It's called *Diners, Drive-ins and Dives: An All-American Road Trip . . . with Recipes!* He published two more Triple D books, in 2009 and 2013. *Guy Fieri Food: Cookin' It, Livin' It, Lovin' It* came out in 2011. It was his first collection of original recipes.

In addition, Fieri has his own clothing line. He has also created a line of kitchen knives. Guy Fieri barbecue sauces, salsas, and ready-to-eat foods are sold in stores.

Fieri has appeared on other Food Network shows. They include *Ultimate Recipe Showdown,* and *Rachael vs. Guy: Celebrity Cook-Off.* He's also served as a guest judge on *Food Network Star.* In 2008, he launched *Guy Off the Hook.* It was filmed in front of a live **audience**.

Fieri thought it would be fun to host a game show. He mentioned this to his manager. It wasn't long before he got a chance! Fieri hosted NBC's *Minute to Win It* from March 2010 through September 2011.

Fieri and fellow
Food Network star
Rachael Ray

Home & Family

Many people want to know if Fieri is really like he appears on television. Most people who meet him agree the answer is "yes."

Fieri often credits his success to the support of his parents, family, and friends. He still lives in Santa Rosa. He built a house for his parents next to his and Lori's home. The Fieri property has a pool and a backyard driveway with skateboard **ramps**. That way his boys can entertain their friends without leaving home.

Of course food is a major part of his home life. He has a huge outdoor kitchen. It includes a barbecue grill and a brick pizza oven.

The family also enjoys dirt-biking vacations. And they often relax at their cabin in the Northern California woods. Sadly, family gatherings are missing Fieri's sister, Morgan. She died in 2011 after a battle with **cancer**.

DID YOU KNOW?
In 2007, Fieri cooked mac and cheese for American troops overseas.

Inspired by Guy Fieri

BBQ Burger Surprise

Serves 4

Ingredients

- **2 strips bacon**
- **2 pounds hamburger meat**
- **8 thin slices of cheese**
- **4 hamburger buns**
- **½ cup barbecue sauce**

1. Ask an adult for help.

2. Cook the bacon. Set it on paper towels to drain.

3. Divide the hamburger meat into eight equal pieces. Roll each piece into a ball. Flatten each ball into a 4-inch-(10 cm) wide patty.

4. Put a slice of cheese on a patty. Break a strip of bacon in half. Put it on the cheese.

5. Add a tablespoon of barbecue sauce. Put a slice of cheese on top.

6. Put another patty on top of the first one. Pinch the edges of the patties together.

7. Repeat steps 4 through 6 with the remaining patties.

8. Heat a frying pan over medium heat. Place the burgers in the pan. Cook them for 4 minutes. Turn the burgers over. Cook them for 4 more minutes.

9. Place the burgers on the buns. Serve with the remaining barbecue sauce. Bite into the burgers with care! The hot cheese inside may spill out.

Giving Back

Fieri believes it is important to give back to the people who made him successful. He supports the police and the military. He has visited military bases around the world to entertain and inspire troops. His support of the US Navy won him an invitation to cook at the White House!

Fieri also spends some of his time to helping parents teach their children healthy eating habits. He worked with California legislators. In 2008, they made the second Saturday in May Cook with Your Kids Day. In 2011, a new resolution passed recognizing Cook with Your Kids Day every Sunday.

In 2010, Fieri launched the Cooking with Kids program to combat childhood **obesity**. In 2013, he and Food Network co-star Rachael Ray partnered on the *Rachael vs. Guy Kids Cook-Off.* That same year, Fieri began hosting the reality series *Guy's Grocery Games.*

Today, Fieri continues to educate kids on healthy eating habits. He urges parents to practice those habits with their kids. *Guy's Big*

Fieri's passion for food and fun comes through in everything he does.

Bite started its seventeenth season in 2014. And *Diners, Drive-ins and Dives*'s twenty-second season started in 2015! Fieri likes to "live big, laugh hard, and cook wild." Those who know him well might say that's just what he does!

Timeline

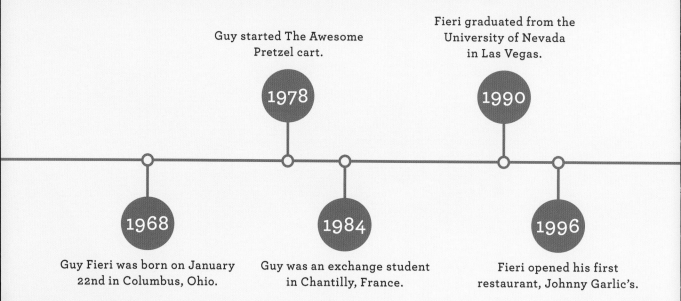

Guy started The Awesome
Pretzel cart.

1978

Fieri graduated from the
University of Nevada
in Las Vegas.

1990

1968

Guy Fieri was born on January
22nd in Columbus, Ohio.

1984

Guy was an exchange student
in Chantilly, France.

1996

Fieri opened his first
restaurant, Johnny Garlic's.

Guy Fieri Says

"We're riding the bus
to Flavortown!"

"If it's funky,
we'll find it."

"Love, peace,
and taco grease!"

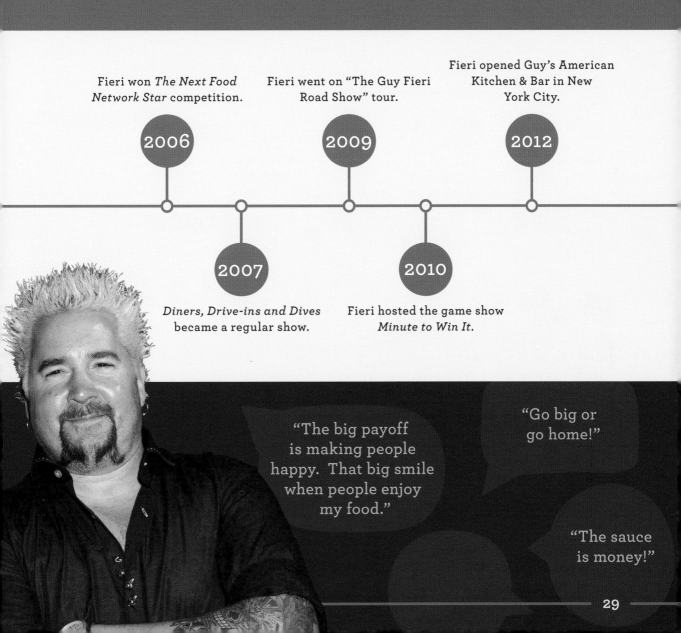

Fieri won *The Next Food Network Star* competition.

2006

Fieri went on "The Guy Fieri Road Show" tour.

2009

Fieri opened Guy's American Kitchen & Bar in New York City.

2012

2007

Diners, Drive-ins and Dives became a regular show.

2010

Fieri hosted the game show *Minute to Win It*.

"The big payoff is making people happy. That big smile when people enjoy my food."

"Go big or go home!"

"The sauce is money!"

Glossary

audience – a group of people watching a performance.

cancer – any of a group of often deadly diseases marked by harmful changes in the normal growth of cells. Cancer can spread and destroy healthy tissues and organs.

concert – a musical performance or show.

cuisine – a way or style of cooking food.

culinary – having to do with the kitchen or cooking.

demonstration – a public display of how to do something or how something works.

episode – one show in a television series.

finalist – one of the last people or teams still competing in a contest or tournament.

hospitality – the business of providing food, drinks, entertainment, and other services.

immigrant – a person who enters another country to live.

obesity – the condition of having too much body fat.

ramp – a sloping surface.

vegetarian – not including any meat, poultry, or fish.

Websites

To learn more about Reality TV Titans, visit **booklinks.abdopublishing.com**. These links are routinely monitored and updated to provide the most current information available.

Index

A

Awesome Pretzel Cart, The, 8, 9

B

birthplace, 6
books, 4, 22
  Diners Drive-ins and Dives: An All-American Road Trip . . . with Recipes!, 22
  Guy Fieri Food: Cookin' It, Livin' It, Lovin' It, 22

C

California, 6, 8, 12, 14, 24, 26
childhood, 6, 7, 8, 9
classic car collection, 20
Cook with Your Kids Day, 26
Cooking with Kids program, 26

D

Diners, Drive-ins and Dives, 4, 18, 20, 22, 27

E

education, 10, 12

F

family
  Ferry, Jim (father), 6, 7, 8, 10, 24
  Ferry, Morgan (sister), 6, 24
  Ferry, Penny (mother), 6, 7, 10, 24
  Fieri, Giuseppe (grandfather), 6
  Fieri, Hunter (son), 12, 24
  Fieri, Lori (wife), 12, 16, 24
  Fieri, Ryder (son), 12, 16, 24
France, 10, 12
Food Network, 4, 16, 18, 22, 26

G

Guy Fieri Road Show, The, 20
Guy Off the Hook, 22
Guy's Big Bite, 17, 26, 27
Guy's Grocery Games, 26

M

military support, 26
Minute to Win It, 22
music, 20

N

Next Food Network Star, The, 16

P

products, 22

R

Rachael vs. Guy Kids Cook-Off, 26
Ray, Rachael, 22, 26
restaurants owned by Guy Fieri, 14, 15, 16
  Guy's American Kitchen & Bar, 15
  Johnny Garlic's California Pasta Grill, 14
  Tex Wasabi's Rock n' Roll Sushi BBQ, 14